Living, Loving, Lasting

— Jessica W. Garwick El-Amin

The Collection

Life's Rhythms Rolled Over Time

by

Jessica Winnie Garwick El-Amin

IGI Press • Minneapolis

Text copyright ©2008 by Jessica El-Amin

All rights reserved. No part of this book may be reproduced, stored in a retrieval system, or transmitted in any form or by any means—electronic, mechanical, photocopying, recording, or otherwise—without the prior written permission of Jessica El-Amin, except for the inclusion of brief quotations in an acknowledged review.

Cover design by www.webs911.com

IGI Press
241 First Avenue North
Minneapolis, MN 55401 U.S.A.

Website address: www.igigraphics.com

Library of Congress Cataloging-in-Publication Data

El-Amin, Jessica Winnie Garwick, 1976-
  The collection : life's rhythms rolled over time / by Jessica Winnie Garwick El-Amin.
     p. cm.
  Poems.
  ISBN 978-0-9799963-2-0
  I. Title.
  PS3605.L13C65 2008
  811'.6--dc22
                                            2008016236

Manufactured in the United States of America
1 2 3 4 5 6 - BP - 13 12 11 10 09 08

With the Name of G-d, The Merciful Benefactor, The Merciful Redeemer

I have always been a poet.
There were years in my life that I allowed my gift to sleep due to the stresses and grief that life laid at my doorstep. When I realized that life's' trials and tribulations are only
A test of faith, my gift reawakened.
I let G-d back into my life, I realized the potential,
That was blown into my lungs when I was born.
The Collection;
inspired by my life of poetry.

I would like to thank my mother and father for always encouraging me to strive for success and happiness.
My family and friends that have made my life full of experiences and adventures to write about.
To my children, my five eyes,
Ishmael Nasir, Idreis Jabreil IbnKhalid, Inayah Nafisah, Ibrahim Noah IbnKhalid and Isa Najee;
Whom fill me with love and patience.
To my cousins and sisters in-life may we forever and always keep climbing for the top.

To my husband, my best-friend, the other half of my brain,
the one who wraps me in his arms,
may we continue to learn and love together.
Truly, we are blessed.

Giving all praises to G-d
For my life and this opportunity
AllahuAkbar, G-d Is The Greatest.

Table of Contents

A Child's Thoughts
- Peace of Mind 10
- A Stars' First Love 11
- The Cabin 12
- Friar's Point, MS 14

Searching
- Our Silent Train 16
- And It Shall Read 18
- Keep On Steppin' 19
- Inspire Me 21
- Fate in Your Hands 23
- The Union 25
- Sweet Dreams 26
- Three Days 'til Twenty-Two 28
- Love Black Power 29

Reflecting
- Hampton Bound 32
- Chasing My Dreams 33
- Ancestors 35
- My Gentle Kiss 36
- Daddy's Angel 38

Motherhood
- Since Carrying You 42
- My Candy Boy 43
- Momma 44
- This is Love 46
- Walden 48

My Thin Line

- Sing To Me Luther 50
- One Stolen Moment 51
- Lost in Your World 54
- The Five L's 55
- Just A Little Taste 56
- A Page from my Journal 58
- Breathless 59
- Fixing my broken heart 60
- Storm Clouds Lifted 62
- Lost Soldier 62
- Loving Words 63
- Baby Girl's Last Cry 64

The Way Lover's Do

- Honey Girl 68
- Yes 70
- Why Beautiful? 72
- Turn On this Love 74
- Foolish Love 77
- Winnie's Gaye Feeling 78
- Soulmates 79
- Wedding Vows 80

Istanbul Memoirs

- The List 82
- Midnight Rain 83
- Ramadan Mubarak 85
- Fajr Idhan 88
- Birlik Sokak, Levent, IST 90

Last Page

- Looking Back 95

Biography

A Child's Thoughts

Peace of Mind
(1988 - 12 years of age)

The day will come
When I can sit down
Rest my feet and let my
Soul take a breath

The world will stand still
And the time will stop ticking

All I dream to get accomplished
Will be done

And I'll have time to give
My mind
A piece of itself

A Stars' First Love
(1989 - 13 years of age)

When a new star is born
A new heart is born also

Never apart the star flies
Through the air like
A loose balloon

But when a star dies
A heart dies also

And the balloon pops

The Cabin
(1991 - 14 years of age)

The hawk circles above me
High up in the sky
Where he is far away from worries
Far away from fears

No one can harm him as he soars through the air

Why can't I be like he
And fly high through the trees

A game of croquet has been started on the lawn
Uncle Jason and me against Kell and Mom
Although we are winning
I hear a whistle
Coming towards me from the trees
Reminding me we are missing
The true champion of the game
He was an artist, but no one would give him his fame
Now gone, his spirit and ash blow in the breeze

I am frightened of making this place in my heart

Although the land is lovely
The creek water pure and the raspberries ripe

I only have the hawk to share the beauty with
We have something in common
My people are absent
I am unaided just like he

In my family there is no one
No other Black beauty to share
The cabin's riches with
No other Black face

So I feel alone
Like the hawk in the sky
It's a shame, I cannot fly

Friar's Point, MS
(1992 - 15 years of age)

The Mississippi Delta calls my name

Whispering in the wind
The fifteen years
That I missed and lost and lied

The Brass Monkey
I bought from the liq in town
Without my picture id
Really fucked me up

And while my head was spinning

I saw you
With your band
Singing and singing
As you hit them notes and your voice
Bellowed throughout Friar's Point, MS.

I laid flowers on your grave
Remembering all the stories I heard about you
I smiled, a tear rolled
I loved you
A love from a daughter
To a father
We both never knew

Searching

Our Silent Train

By the light of the moon
As it watches over the evenings' night
We wait patiently
Next move is unknown
Listen close
Hear my peoples' moans

Bodies and minds are full of fright
Yet none comparable to what we've left behind
We are the box cars with souls
As we continue this everlasting fight

Some of the great ones have led us
The Moses of America's past
Waiting for the river to take us north
So we may cry out
Free at last, free at last!!

You will never hear the whistle of our train
We move in silence
Leaving behind the master's violence
Trying to erase our memories pains

At times you may hear our echoes
Or feel our spirits moving in the wind
But one, Freedom
The other, Death
Will soon be destinies end.
The kitchen and cotton we will no longer tend

You may even be lucky enough
To catch a glimpse of the field hand
Or house slave's ghost
As we move our way through the tree brush
To the chest we treasure the most

We are on freedom's journey
Blessed with G-d's will
Taking each step cautiously
As America's saga of being built
Slowly unfolds
We continue our divine journey
On the Underground Railroad.

And It Shall Read

Bury me with roses
For I am a flower
That refuses to stop growing

Bury me with roses
Please lay a red rose at my feet
For my foundation was built on love

Bury me with roses
For I am a garden
That has spread my seeds
To each of you and now you may grow as well

Bury me with roses
Please lay a black rose across my heart
For my love for each of you is
Strong and for an eternity

Bury me with roses
For I am one of G-d's blossoms
Who has touched all of your lives
Please lay a white rose above my head
For now I am on my journey home

Bury me with roses
Do not weep, do not shed a tear
My time was long and dear
Our journey is not over,
My earthly body is laid to rest
My mind at ease and my soul set free

Keep On Steppin'

Don't ever let them get you down
Never let the man
Turn your smile, into a frown
You have way too much at stake
Struggle now
Can't be afraid to open the door
Decide your own fate
No matter what
Life throws your way
To make you feel sad and blue
Keep On Steppin'
Ask G-d, to put the strength inside of you

Keep your head up
Your eyes on the prize
Make your mark on this world
First place is yours, don't ever compromise
Some days seem long, it will be a fight
Keep On Steppin'
Ask G-d, to bring the sunshine and
Put away the dark of the night

When days seem long
And the path you thought was right
Turns out to be wrong
Don't hang your head low, lift up your chin

Find a new path to begin
No matter what the trials and tribulations
He puts your way
Close your eyes, bow your head, lift your hands,
And pray for his word is always true
If no one else he believes in you

Inspire Me

I . . .
Inspiration begin with I
I . . .
Am the only one who can free the chains
That life has placed on me
When all around seems to tumble and fall
I have to be the one
To still stand tall
And always give myself my all and all
I . . . Inspiration begins with I . . .

G-d made it this way from the start
When he put the womb of the world in our hearts
Here is where the sun gets its shine
And why the stars in the sky
Twinkle all the time
Here is where rock gets its roll
And rap its rhyme
Surely, you know what's on my mind
The Black Woman
So precious and one of a kind
I . . . Inspiration begins with I . . .

No time for us to hang our head
Our Black children have to be fed
No time for us to slip through the crack
Our Black men need to lean on our backs
We are the beginning and end of the alphabet

From one until infinity
Black Women we started this
We'll be here until eternity
Surely, you know what my eyes see
The Black Woman she lives inside of me
I... Inspiration begins with I

Don't need no man by our sides to be strong
Don't need a coaster to ride
We can do bad all alone
We wait for the day
For you to put us back on the throne
'Til then . . .
We'll handle this shit on our own
And rise to the occasion
I . . . . Inspiration begins with I

Close my eyes
Put my life in the Almighty's hands
For he alone gives me all future plans
Here is where I place my trust
He never complains
I'm always on his mind
And this brotha he never puts up a fuss
It's no infatuation true love he has for me
That is why he gives me the strength
To put inspire inside of me

Fate in Your Hands

I want to lay down inside
Your pearly gates
Feel safe
In your hands is where I put my fate
While I'm here on your earth
Thanking you
For my birth
Wondering when it's my turn
To come home
To your kingdom never feel alone

I suppose Martin
Found his mountain top at your front door
And brotha Tupac
He don't have to be a thug no more
Off to a better space
Home to our heavenly place
Guess it's the only date
We never get to break

C'mon my Lord
You can tell...
This place where I'm living
Is it hell?
My brothers are dying
The man keeps on lying
And the babies even you
You can her them crying

I'll tell Nikki
Her big brother sends his love
There's no better place for
Him to rest his head
Than in your heavenly bed up above

Five steps . . . is much too long for me
I just wanta take one
And then fall into your arms
Where the devil,
He can do no wrong

Until the angels take me higher
And I see my dad and baby again
I'll continue on the path
You've laid me on
My earthly friend
And when you
Call my name I'll answer,
"Yes, I'm ready."
Then all will be done
I'll lay down inside those gates
Feel safe
In your hands is where I put my faith.

The Union

Black Men
So Strong
Yet so damn weak
Need a Black Woman
At your side
To be complete

Black Men
So smart
Yet so dumb founded
Need a Black Woman
At your side
To keep you whole and grounded

Black Men
Such kings
But still such slaves
Walking round smiling with
All these caves......
Need a Black Woman
So your soul can be saved

Black men dying
Black women crying
We gotta wake up
Our nation is dying
African Black Negro Colored American People

Sweet Dreams

All this stress, no time to rest
I close my eyes, take a breathe, and sigh
I get a second to break
A minute to take
Wish I was sleep
Too many things to peep
No time for me
In all this madness, I still ain't free

Worried about yesterday
Today's full of sorrow
Hell, I'm already scared of tomorrow
Life's clock don't stop, it just ticks
Tick Tock... Tick Tock...
Gotta keep on... keeping on
Can't let it beat me
Ain't never been one for letting life's things defeat me
If my dreams could talk, they'd have a speech
Only they can really see
Yeah...My dreams
My sweet, sweet dreams
An avenging angel they'd birth if they could conceive

If only I could take a seat
Rest my weary feet
Catch my breathe, relax for awhile
Maybe get a chance to even smile
Then again, can't be caught sleeping
Gotta be ready for life's next beating

Don't want to be sitting
Can't be too demanding, when life throws
Its next blow, I wanta be standing

This ride I'm on, sho' aint steady
Always ripping and running
Now realizing, I gotta get my soul ready
Trial after trial, Same ole' song
Some days, I can't wait for paradise, my after life
This game is getting much too long
Finally think my purpose is strong
At least enough to fight
But life...
Life comes raging through the night
Do I know where I stand in this chaotic land?
Are my feet concrete?
Shit, I wish I could make life take a seat

Listening?
You'd probably think I'm depressed
Not at all I just need some rest
Let my mind lay down, Let my soul sway
And may my heart please get time to pray
I'd give anything for a second out of the day
To let my dreams come out and play,
Oh, they'd be So Sweet

Three Days 'til Twenty-Two

Got that feeling again,
Don't want my life to end
Fills my insides like a ghost
I can't move
Time on this earth is
What I value most
When is the end?
Begins and stops in a blink
Got this feeling again
Races through my soul
Into the depths of my bones
Out of my control
Never imagined being this
Scared to go home
Hurts the most to know
They'll be a day
When the moon
Goes away
And I won't see the sun
And I'll be gone to stay

Love Black Power

Have you gazed into a Black man's soul?
Have you see the strength in which he holds?
Look into his eyes one day
For there you'll find a king
Who wants to come out and play
Embrace his body and you'll see
A man of great power and prestige
Hold his heart in your hand
Stand by his side for he is
Your honor and your man
Be his two feet on which to walk
Be his lips on which he talks
Be his shoulders on which he can lean
For you my sister
Are his African Queen

Reflecting

Hampton Bound
Hampton, VA

I have myself
This is why I don't need anyone by my side
I was raised to be my own guide
Know how to survive
Chin up now!

I have my pride
Not one that someone handed to me
I gave birth to it many years ago
And now it's helping me grow into
The woman I am becoming
Chest out now!

I have a sense of direction
And know which path to take
And which road leads
To my dreams

My hands are open waiting to receive the world

Chasing My Dreams

Remember when the wind blew that dollar bill out of your hand?
And every time you thought you...
Almost... had it
The wind blew again

Feels like how I'm chasing my dreams

Each road I take turns into a dead end
Although I thought I had the master plan
But failed once again, and after my pride mends
Lift up my chin, pick up my face
Continue on life's never-ending race

Hope this time I get the gold
All these ambitions and goals
Inside wondering how my story will unfold
But only the creator really knows
What path he's placed me on
Fighting the gifts blessed inside
While I'm trippin' and slippin' on this crazy ride
See the season's change as I do the same
Yet I feel so trapped inside this chaotic game

Chasing my dreams
Like a crack fiend cooks that powder
Chasing my dreams one of G-d's daughter
Chasing my dreams as they cry out louder and louder

Open my eyes now... when I pray
Maybe then I'll see what I've been missing
Open my ears so when G-d speaks
He knows that I'm listening.

Chasing my dreams
But they keep blowing in the wind
I gotta chase my dreams
So this madness will end

Ancestors

Sitting on the sun
Only time
I'll ever get
To be a
Star
Travel the world
From here to afar
Setting with the horizon
I spread my arms
Around the world
Keeping warm my children
All the brown boys and girls
Take a ride
Up on my rainbow
Dip into my pot of gold
For here is where
Our ancestors' secrets
Will finally be untold
Sitting on the Sun

My Gentle Kiss

Two hundred seventy days I spent with thee
After the ninth month, birthed from the womb
I was finally free
Lay to rest on my mother's breast
But the strength of your arms
Could not be found
Something missing I could not believe
Without your seed
Daddy I would not have been conceived.

First steps, tooth, and birthday did you miss
Yet G-d still brought your gentle kiss
He placed it on my soul
Give thanks to him daily for now my spirit glows
Like the sun when it rises from its horizon

Although were are so far apart
This earth depart G-d sent you home
I have always known from the start
When I miss you to look into the depths of my heart
For the air I breathe it came from you
So I no longer feel blue

I go searching for you in my dreams
You left a piece behind
A baby girl, a daughter so precious and genuine
Don't fret daddy
We shall meet again in due time

There are days that I long for you
My heart is dry
And only tears pour from my swollen eyes
I close them... and feel you here at my side
A father in which to confide

I feel free
I close them
And reminisce to the time I spent with thee
And I thank G-d for that gentle kiss
That part of you
He let stay with me

Daddy's Angel
Greensboro, NC

If I could recall how my father use to smile
It would fit your lips to a tee
The more I open my eyes
The clearer it is to see
The Lord above has sent you to me

If I could remember how he use to listen
While my mouth ran and did all its' talking
It would be your ears
That heard all the gentle words
That came from deep within my heart
Although this earth depart
Somehow now I don't feel like
We are so far apart

You are an inspiration
The way I wish my daddy could be
Although his planted seed
Has grown into a beautiful flower
My soul and roots
Still need to be watered

Thank G-d daily
For a man like you in my life
You make the wrong things seem right
You keep me on track the way he would want
And little do you know
My broken heart you help to mend
For you are watching over me most
By being my friend

If I had my father figure
He would have your invisible wings
Daddy's Angel you are truly a blessing

Motherhood

Since Carrying You

Laying here in bed
Missing you
I hear a baby's voice crying out for me
In the distance
Yearning for my touch
In the distance
I see your face in my dreams

As I lay here and rock myself to sleep

I think of holding you
As you lay your tender head
Upon my breast and drift away to sleep
As I sing the lullabies my mother
Used to sing to me

Laying here in bed
Listening to that baby's voice crying
Crying out for me
Far off in the distance

I never wanted to let you go
No time now no where for us to go
Just wait for me please
At our special place
And come my way again
We'll have time I hope
Later in life for you to be my child, my friend

My Candy Boy

Young caramel full of son
The name I call you
Sweet sunshine that wakes me
In the morning
Love to spend my whole day
Watching you learn
Teaching you to be better
Than myself

Fat cheeks full of sugar
That I steal
Every time I place my lips upon them
My little patience maker
You pitter patter over my mind
In and out of my energy
Walking over my body
In and out of my mental peace

I watch you while you sleep
And the smile
Coming from your dreams is me
True love that only
Us two share
Little caramel full of sun

Momma

I need you like the moon needs the sun
Yearn for the day to be with you again
Hold me in your arms
Sing to me like you did when I was young
I'm walking these Hampton shores alone
And you're not here
The love we share that's oh so dear
I miss you
Only wish I had the words to tell you so
Until we are in union
I close my eyes
I feel you here by my side
Telling me all the things I need to know
All the places I need to go
You've put inside

So I close my eyes

Feel so alone in this cold world
Full of chaos and lies
With you so far away now all I do is pray
For the day to see you again
My mother my best-friend
So many miles away
So all I do is spend my day
Wishing you were here with me
Only you bring all the unconditional love

That I'll ever need
Then reality hits
When I open my eyes and look around
You're not here
My smile turns to a frown
Sitting in the dorm
So I, close my eyes

Many decisions now to make, so many
Roads in front to take
Hope I pick the one
I feel you deep down inside
Telling me all the things I need to know
All the places I need to go
You've put inside
So I, close my eyes,
 I feel you here by my side
And I miss you so
How much...???
Will you ever know?
It's so hard with you not here
The love we share
That's oh so dear
And I miss you momma
Don't know when we'll meet again
My love, my best friend
So I, close my eyes

This is Love

Today tears overflowed my soul
Flooded my body from my toes
To the very end of my split ends
A joyful
Sad cry that would
Not flow from my eyes
Because I was oh so proud of you
There would be
So many more times
I would have to leave you
Today had to be a very successful good-bye

So strong
We forgot to kiss each other
We so independent
My little man
Do you ever imagine to be?
The little man you are.

Sitting here staring out of glass
At this day
Missing you already
The count would be endless of
The times I've already thought of you
And its only nine o two

Your hazel, chestnut brown
Golden locks so intertwined
Your brown eyes so pretty as they
Stare into mine
No greater love can there be than this

Walden
Storrs, CT

Raining on the outside
Breakfast cooking patiently
Missing you
Tears fill my eyes
But refuse to fall
"You have to be strong"
I hear you say inside my mind
Nice shower
Still keeping me warm
Like a newborn in his crib
Wish your grandson would
Remove his foot from my rib
Twenty two in eight
Another date we never break
Missing you
Breakfast cooking patiently
As Sweet Honey
Fills the room

My Thin Line

Sing To Me Luther

When I finally choose
To open my eyes
I saw you standing there
Just as clear as pure water in a glass
You smile at me
Whisper sweet nothings
That I can't hear
I love the way your voice
Lied through your lips
I see you
Looking so fine
Got me dreaming
This time hoping...
You were really mine
Wishing I could hold you
Not wonder where you'd been
Or who it was you were doing
Or had already done
Even if it was now dawn
Just glad you were here
And that I was the one
You shared a house with
Even though I wished it was a home

One Stolen Moment

Thoughts of you fill the air
Smoke clouds raise their eyes
Try again
The baby cries

Love opens its wings
I get wrapped inside
One more chance
No more lies
Please
Can I run away and hide?

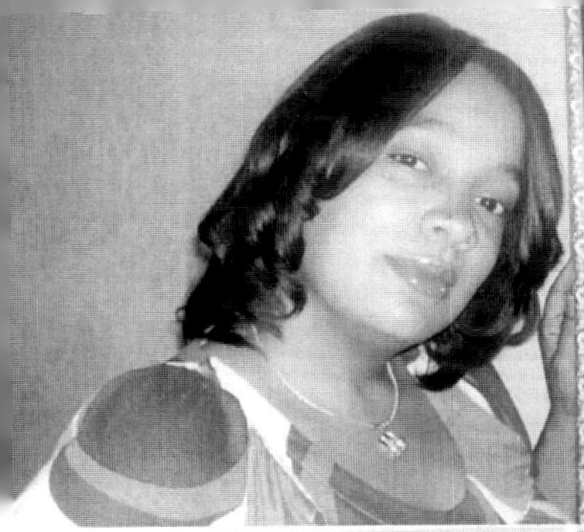
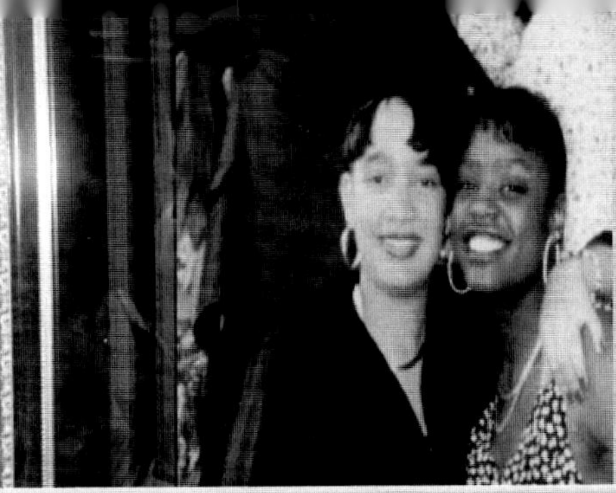
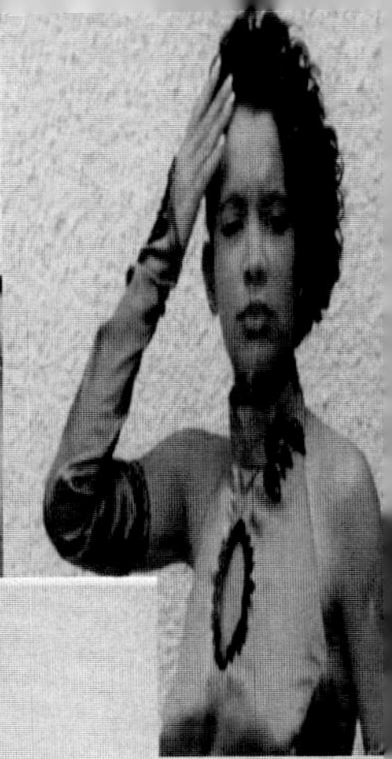
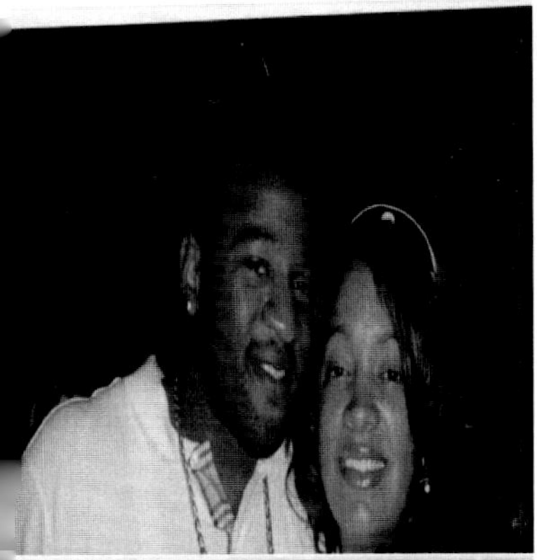
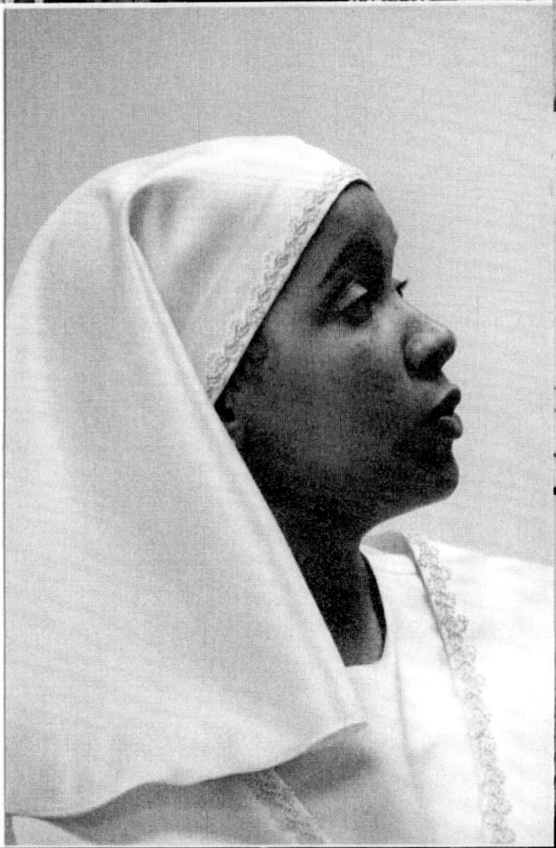
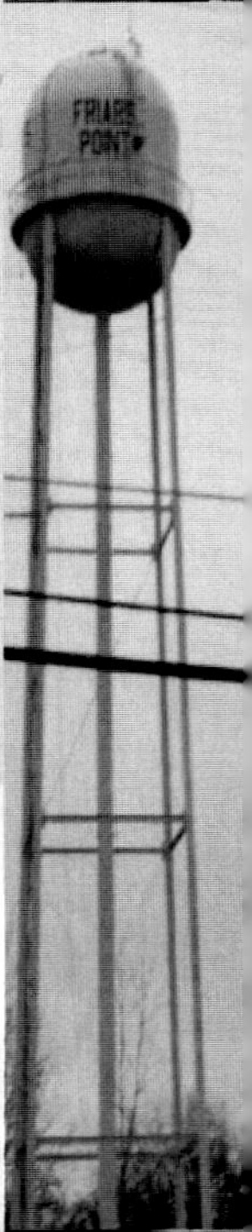
FRIARS
POINT
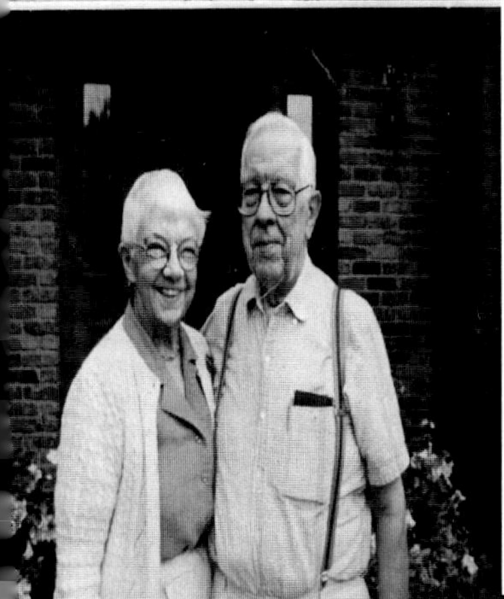
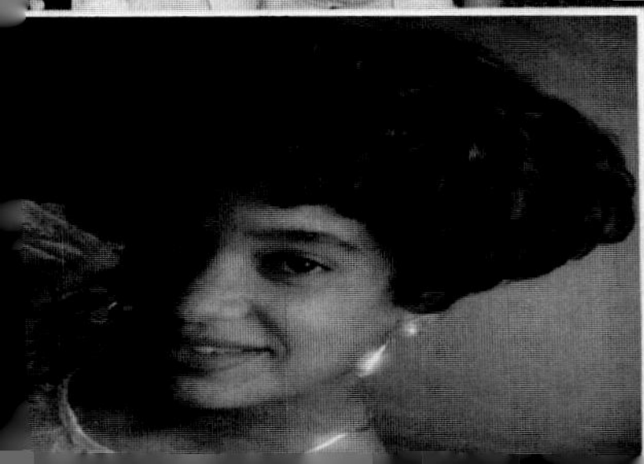
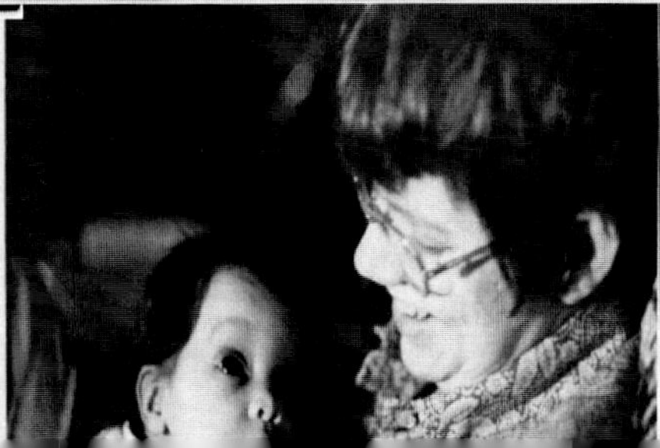
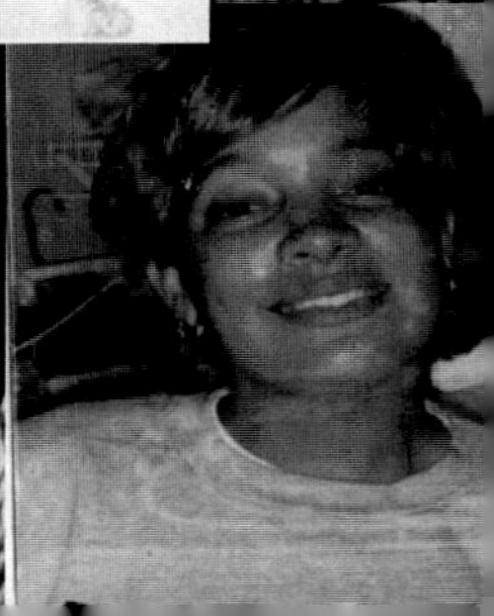

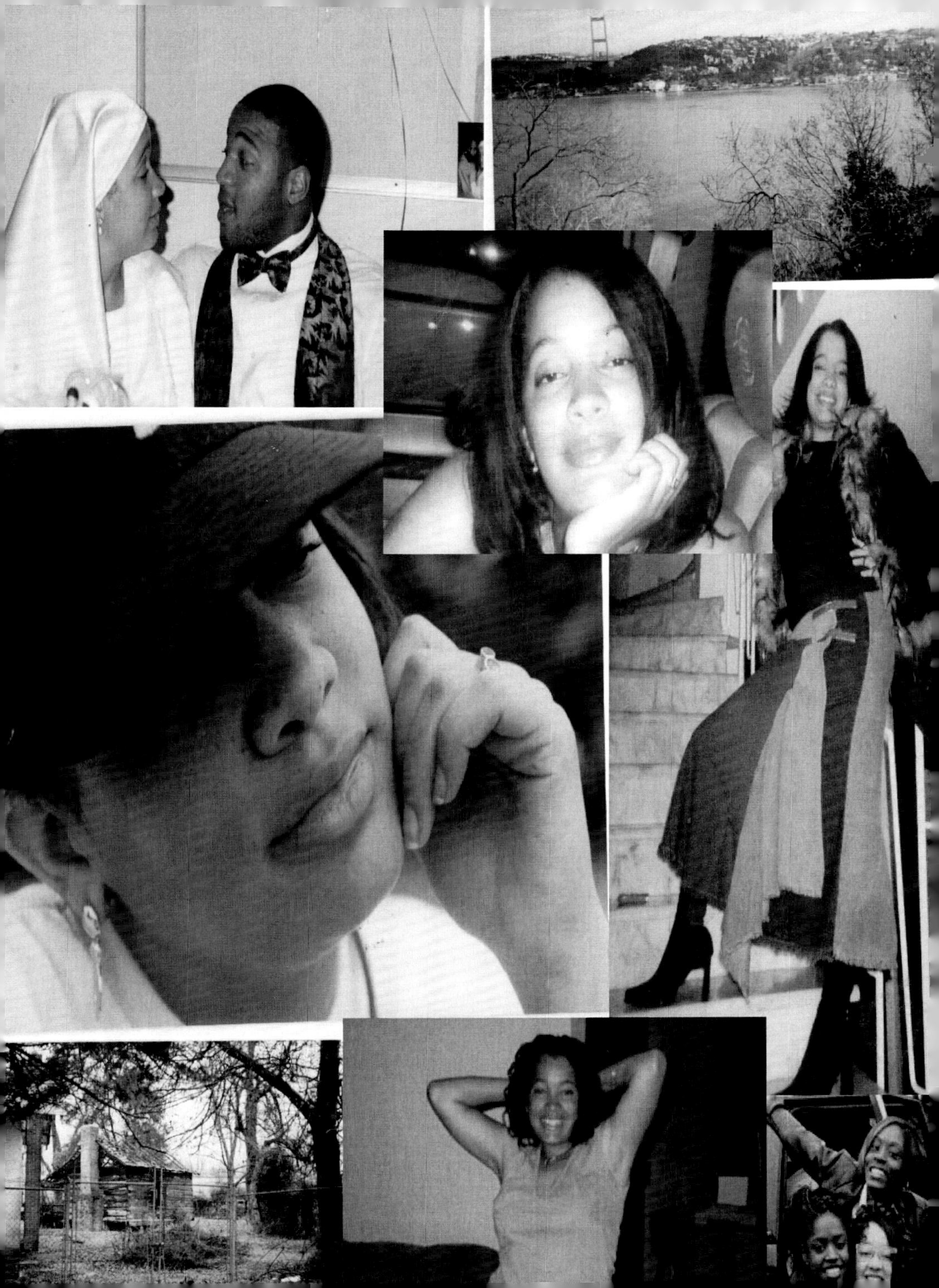

Lost in Your World

Are you happy?
When you look into my eyes
When you lay your head between my thighs
After you eat and I clean your plate
At 4:00 am in the morning when
You promised you wouldn't be late
When the phone rings and the pager beeps
And it's not me
Are you smiling?
It's obvious that this isn't working
And someone needs to leave
You don't respect me
Threw me on the ground twice
My body against the wall
Grabbed my neck
Bruised my arm
Ankles bloody now
All over some fucking keys
So you could leave to run the streets
Are you happy?
Lost in my own river
That flows through my own bones
All for my love jones
When I don't ask for more
Than trust, love and honesty,
You do your thang
In time you'll see
When you're alone somewhere
Looking for me.

The Five L's

Losing the love that once filled my soul with joy
Loving you for so many things
Leaving love behind with the pain you caused my life
Letting myself go trying to love you
Learning there is more to life than love

Losing my dreams helping you reach yours
Loving the way we used to love one another
Leaving you is not something easy for me to do
Letting go of the past is very hard
Learning to live my life without you

Losing the trust that I had but that you never let me have
Loving you through all the ups and downs
Leaving isn't always the answer
Letting my expectations suffer for the love of a man
Learning that G-d is more than everything we share

Losing respect for you because of you
Loving life more without you around
Leaving my fears of being without you
Letting my eyes open to see all that I have in store
Learning to love myself more than I love you

Losing isn't something I want to do
Loving myself is most important
Leaving you behind
Letting go, moving forward with my life
Learning how to love again.

Just A Little Taste

I'm drowning in my tears
My lips reach up out of the
Crystal clear pool of blood
That I have shed
To catch a breathe

Souls cry out for an innocence
That was rebuilt only
To be shattered and lost
Only to be broken again
To be broken down
By your manhood, your boyhood
That once gave life
Which now breeds death into
This love affair we once shared

My heart drowning too
In a river of tears
That flow from out
Of the depths of my soul
Crying out aching heart
With no place to go
Reaching out to you
To stop the draining of its' soul

It races out of me
As my mind sweats out all of the
Vivid memories of the pain
That carried my life away
Into what it is today

On this day
When things still aren't the same
Just want to breathe again
And exhale the wind
Just want to taste the sweet
Sweet taste of love
That we once shared

A Page from my Journal

I wonder why the Black woman is so wrapped
Up in her family while
The Black man is so consumed by
The world around him

I heard this song and it
Said, "If only this world
would let me go
I could love you like I know I should"

So you gonna let these
Street fools and these hungry hos,
Destroy our lives, eat your alive?
While you make me sit back
And watch you unfold
There is one thing you still have to learn
You ain't shit without your family
We are the backbone
The only ones there in the end

You must have not crossed that
Path quite yet
Only being twenty years young
But you are so far from stupid
You sure ain't no fool
You have common sense and lots of goals
Know the difference between
Right and wrong, your momma taught you long ago
So why do you do what you do?

Only if you would let this world go
You could show me how much you love me

Breathless

I should have listened closer
When the Prince said he,
"Needed another lover
Like I need a hole in my head".

I am still releasing bullets
Out of myself
Got your gun going off inside of me
Wish I could pull your pistol apart
And wrap it around your throat
Take the breath
You took from my womb
Before it had life
See what your love does to me?

Loving you is like my untied shoe
Gotta keep on reaching down
And every time I do
My hands don't clap
Like they used to
Got my soul iced over frozen solid
Like the jumper you shoot
Now all they
Do is this all they do is . . .

Wonder why
You even open your mouth to tell another lie
I should take the air
you breathe, put it in my lungs,
hold my lips shut
And let you choke

Fixing my broken heart

Sitting here inside myself
Ain't got no rhymes from out my mouth
But this is my freestyle
I am a poetic child

I always try to keep it real
These brothas out here are
Scared of this bomb ass deal

The NBA will never pay you what
My meal is ever worth
Because the love I have for you
Is nothing but true
And the game you love to play
And sometimes loose
Can't even compete
I'm trump tight you see
And I thought you loved me?

Got this other brother that I'm breaking
Off something proper
He's acting like he wants a confrontation
It must be his imagination,
A big exaggeration
Because this isn't nothing more
Than an infatuation

Keep my tea cup warm at
Three in the morn
When I get tired I send you back home
The things I do for you really ain't shit
Your on my time, my tip, I decide when you hit

Thought you was in control?
So I'ma dip out and roll my own flow
Two's comfort and three is definitely
A crowd, but I'll lick them seven digits
When I want to get it hard

'Til then, in the meantime,
My in between time
While your doing your thing
You missing out
On a bomb ass friend
A real woman, a lover
Who's down until the very end

Yah'll scary uncommitted men kill me
Over and over again
And my list of rules and regulations
I continue to bend
Them days is over, don't need no man
Alone is how I mend.

Storm Clouds Lifted

Can't let go of this storm
Rains
Sun comes out the next day
But shit is still the same
Me loving you
You loving yourself

Lost Soldier

Where have you gone?
Strong hunter
Lost in this world
The one that belongs to your man
Can't see you anymore
Misplaced along the road

Loving Words

The saying, "love is blind"
Comes from the idea of doing and being
Everything for love
You become unaware and "blind" of things
That happen around you
The love feels so right that you put it before yourself
Love becomes the priority
You lead your life with the focus of love
Walking, breathing, living, running around in a reality
Actually a state of confusion
All in the name of love
And when love does you wrong,
Your life freezes for that moment
You try to imagine what you did wrong
For love to do you wrong
And yet still even with a broken heart
You will do everything for love
So when people say, "love is blind"
It's not because love can't see
It's because love puts your mind and soul
In a state of shock
That makes you act and behave in a manner
That gives the illusion of not seeing
What is happening around you
And to your own being
Because of love

Baby Girl's Last Cry

Your blues ain't like mine, waiting for the sun to shine,
Inside the skies turn gray.
Patiently preserving,
Waiting for the things I'm deserving.
Longing for the day
All my worries go away.

Don't need to touch you
Or see you with my eyes,
Your divinity is
Why my tears cry, then smile,
Frowning back at me.

Feel like singing,
"Shoo fly don't bother me"
Get that buzzing out my ear,
Stop whispering all those lies
I don't want to hear.

I need to put on a Mary song
And get to stomping my feet.
Testifying up in here
'Bout the shit you done to me.
Shoo fly don't bother me,

Following me, not allowing me.
Rather be striving than denying me.
All that buzzing in my ear,
Back stabbing, back biting me.
Telling me things I don't want to hear.

Like I should be on Brewster's place.
Naked in the tub,
Having my hair washed and
My soul scrubbed.

Shoo fly don't bother me
Making my skin itch, my nose twitch.
Don't you see you're in my space
Touching my face, you wanta' feel my grace?
Get yo' ass outta here !!

It takes pain to make things go away.
You have to lose your sight to see,
And change ain't always good,
But it's what I need.

Your blues ain't like mine

The Way Lover's Do

Honey Girl

At first stroke my vibe
Puts a crick in your neck
Races down your spine
And ripples all through your back

My inner love births itself
Into your determined, stable, beautiful black mind
As my love soothes and comforts you
Your brain starts to unwind

You won't ask for much but my outer touch
Will teach you more than
Any scholar could learn
In an entire lifetime
As my being caresses your soul
Like that nipple in your mouth
When you were four months old

First contact
Leaves you in a state of shock
Put your thoughts in mind cuffs
Leave you whipped and your body on lock

An aurora that reminds you of how things
Used to be naked in our kingdom
Side by side... you and me... pure royalty
Come fill me with your seed
Let's continue the prophecy

I am the mistress of fate
The queen of destiny
Hurry up Now... Jump on Board Now...
Don't let it get too late

You know my love
That love that never goes rotten
Surely never forgotten
So strong...So strong
I'll smoke you up like chronic
In my favorite bong

I am the game you never win
But insist on playing ova' and ova' again
Like that missing piece
That maze that keeps you lost
I'm on fire your desire
Your soul and spirit I'll defrost

Still that puzzle you won't ever put together
So don't ponder don't even try to wonder...???
It would only be a waste
See my heart
It's on that survival chase

I thought you knew I am the woman
Others can only strive to be
Single and Free
And Oh... Oh so in love with me
You know phenomenal Maya
Winnie Oprah Mary
Lauryn Soujouner Coretta Scott King
We come from a place called Africa
The Queens

I got that vibe that loves to foster
I Live On I Stay Strong
And you know I'll always Prosper

Yes

I must confess minds telling me yes
Ever since I rested my lips upon your chest
Confusion got me going
On one of those wild rides
Makes me wanta hold on
You know that ride the kind you wanta jump on
Bud up to the front of line on... Ride on
Let it race down your spine and ride on ride on.

I got this crazed situation
Mad confrontation
Gotta wipe off my forehead
So much perspiration

Just wanta lay down wrap my body surround as
You turn around this frown
Put my head on your chest
Lay your cheek on my thigh and rest
Soak you up put an end to my stress
Let me ease into your body hold your soul in
The palm of my hands
Maybe even make you my man
We can always compromise,
But for now, sit back, and let this temperature rise

Can't pinpoint this one
Seemed as natural as the rising sun
At first only an imagination
Never thought it would be done
And now our day has begun
Caught myself daydreaming bout you
The feeling was kinda strong
I guess I never realized

It could ever be wrong
Sitting here restless
Can't get you out my mind
Guess I'll see if you're 'bout
Something real in due time

Don't want to be just a broad that you knocked
Don't want to feel like I'm on your clock
Just don't wanta make it a sex you up thang
It's my heart that needs the orgasm
Make me sing
A 30 second, body locking, back breaking fuck fling
A do me baby bump'n grind
Is the last thing I need
It's my soul I want you to feed
Not the honey in my panties

Just want you to listen while I'm talking
Run while I'm walking
Be there when I need someone to be jocking
It's you that I want to lock-in
Deep inside the inner depths of me
Can you feel it? Do you see?

Feel like this one is out of my hands
Out on a limb
Somewhere... someone has a master plan
Outta my control so...
I'ma lay back and go with this flow
Listen to our rhythm as the bass blows
On and on into the night
We both know this melody is right
And this vibe...this vibe is oh so tight
Like an angel in flight
I'm listening I must confess
I'm listening to my mind
It's telling me yes.

Why Beautiful?

Why do the butterflies
Decide to fly
Every time I gaze into your deep brown eyes

Am I living a lie?
Or is it the piece of pie
That you get to taste over and over again
Satisfying the wanting you have for me
But when I wake up in the morning
Was it a waste of my sexual soul?
You're not my man, more than a one night stand
We are nothing more than fucking friends

Why do the butterflies
Decide to roam
Every time I hang up the phone I miss your voice
The way you make me laugh
I don't want to be a thing of the past
Are things moving too fast?
Or is it the piece of ass
You get to tap night after night
But I'm not your woman
And that aint right
It aint right, it aint right

Why do the butterflies flutter
Every time I break you off
You know it like Next do
This butta love I share with you
Scared to open this door
I guess it's that ego, that brotha pride
Holding you back afraid to commit

Got these butterflies
Inside
Why.

Turn On this Love

Got all these feelings inside,
With no place to go
I only need a minute of your time,
So I can let you know

From the first time our eyes made love
The feelings began...
I knew inside that you may be the one
But as time has passed you've disappeared
Like the sun when the night falls
And now I sit here and wonder...
Gazing at the moon

My five hour drives, my road trips
I guess they don't mean shit
Cuz' your plans are at the top of your list
Ain't got no time for this stress
Sit back and chill
Remove this headache from my mind
If only you knew like I know
True love takes time
It's exactly what you could find
Take this ride with me

I give you a hundred percent
But can't get ten dimes in return
Tell myself over and over again
That I'm through loving you
Until I hear the ring
And it's you on the line

A smile comes to my face
I want to be yours and you mine

You better recognize
You have a prize in me
Before I float along with this fall breeze
No love lost but none gained
When we hang up the phone
Pain rushes through my veins
Wonder why I go over this with you
Time and time again and again
I don't understand all this mess
Just a test

I'm only here to give you my best
And even then it's not enough
You gotta play the macho role
You gotta be tough, like you don't like it rough

So much I want to give
Have too much of my life left to live
To be bothered with this bullshit

Just want your respect, love and consideration
Us two together we could build a nation
Show some admiration
It's you I want don't have to think twice
Aint no hesitating

A strong woman by your side
What more could you ask for
A best friend in which to confide
Better open your eyes and realize
Want you to place your heart in my hands

Want to be your woman and you my man
Want to share my dreams
Let you know my plans
I want a best friend not just a man

Baby can't you see
Everything you ever wanted
It starts right here with me

I want to put my trust in you
Make me smile
When life's got me down and feeling blu
Just like a queen do
I want to run away into your arms
Where no one else can do me harm

I got all these feelings inside
With no place to go
I only need a minute of your time
So I can let you know

We need to turn this love on.

Foolish Love

Being a fool for love
This is when you act foolish or get treated as a fool
Because of love
Like being taken for granted of or lied to or cheated on
So that you end up looking like a fool
It's when you go around
Knowing your lover lays it down
And somehow it
Becomes a normal feeling for you
And you're the biggest fool when you lose your child
Because of an STD
But the fool
You have become begs you to stay because
You are a fool for love
And when that's still not enough
There are some, who have your husband's blood
But not your DNA
Like Bush smelling Fahrenheit
You can fool me
Once
How's that go? I'm in love
Wondering, Why?
Like them fools do

Winnie's Gaye Feeling

I would fill this page
With my sorrows
Just wake me with the sun
Tomorrow so I know that I
Did all that could be done
Can't keep dodging down
This one way
Don't want to die knowing
I just kept on trying
To find the passion once found in you
Now last
In your world
No longer something we share
Just a feeling
That comes and goes
After making love to you
What's the point in trying?
Just to continue with your lying
While I'm tormented
Just to say
I'm loving you
When that's just a given
And I'm steady fake a smiling
For years it seems
I've been denying
All for the love
For the love of you

Soulmates

Whenever you think of me
Know that I'm thinking of you

And when tears fill your eyes
I'm wiping mine away too

Because what you feel
Is a mirrored emotion for me

It's the union we share
When souls connect

The way ours do

Now I can't tell you how to live your life
But I know where you've been

Because it's me whose walked
The path with you

Our footprints in the sand

I only wish to walk eternity
Holding hand in hand
Souls intertwined
Living out his plan

Wedding Vows

Today is the day
I dedicate my love to you
Come walk on this path with me
Fulfilled with trust, respect, and dignity

Though some may struggle
And some may fall
My pledge to you is to remain strong
Through all and all
For I am you and you are me
Which on this day makes us we

Today is the day

I dedicate my strength to you
Come walk on this path with me
Fulfilled with understanding, communication and honesty

When I look at you
It is my soul mate
Staring back
It's what you see
The one Allah has made for me
More than husband and wife
The warmth he wrapped us in
My best friend
You are truly a blessing in my life
My garment the one on the other side
Half my faith
Today is our day

Istanbul Memoirs

The List
Istanbul

Granola bars . . .
Taco seasoning . . .
Cake mixes . . .
Brownie mix . . .
Did I already say Captain Crunch

Camera
Tape recorder

Betty Crocker makes some choc chip cookie dough

Pancake mix and syrup so maybe bring four

Also Velveeta cheese and
Grits
Oatmeal
Cornbread mix

Lawry's salt
Bbque sauce

Is Randy bringing his guitar? I know it is not possible but
Ishmael would
Love
His

Just a short email of all the things that we miss
Please, please send them
Quick

Midnight Rain

A storm's mystery nature's history
A timeline
Thunder claps as lightening slaps
Its own hip hop beat
Lightening claps as thunder slaps
Its own hip hop beat

Wind blows the rain around
Creating a whistling sound
That awakens sweet baby slumber
Cold air creeps through the window cracks
But I hear you sneaking in a quiet song

Rain rushes down the hills through the streets
Water gushes from the sewers feet
Draining
Cleansing the day's filth away

Glass shakes winds breathe so strong
Laying hoping nothing breaks
As I feel the air move around
Storms arms very long
Close my eyes try to find my dream
But all I can hear is music
From clouds bursting
Trees thirsting for a drink

Praying while I'm laying
Dirty little orphan boy isn't too wet and cold
He was already shivering
Hours ago while the wind blowed

Son's awake, "I heard a loud sound, Mom !?".
Look outside
"Wow, the rain is really coming down".
Lay by me I'll sing you back to sleep
Singing in the rain the drops blow
A voice of love ballads
As the drips roll down the pane
Swimming, looking
Searching to find a mate

Baby sleeping sound, belly full
Clock keeps going around
I can't sleep now, so many noises in my ears
Filling my head with sound
Quiet outside inside the water still moves
The splish splash of my mop
The running toilet downstairs
Suds as they hit the floor
Storms moved on
Beautiful sky reminds me who keeps things alive
The one we fear the one who we hold dear
The Creator, the Rainmaker
The Rain,
Maker of this beautiful musical piece

Ramadan Mubarak

There is no feeling quite like this
In the world
If you ever experienced it for the first time
How could you not
Want to practice
Al-Islam

To wake up in the dawn
When light just begins to touch the sky
At first you are almost sleep walking
You maybe use the bathroom
Before stumbling down the stairs

Drink water
Rushes through your mind a thousand times
And you do
Drink

This morning I had eggs with tomatoes, yogurt with raisins
and honey, a piece of turkey
And more water
I put my dishes away and grabbed a half of banana
I'm a breastfeeding mother
It may be a long day of fasting a little over 12 hours

I make wudu
My hands, my face, still chewing the banana
My arms, my neck and ears
Savoring the last taste of food until dusk
As I rinse my mouth three times

I remember the taste of water
My last refreshment
Walk back upstairs
Fix my hijab and enter
The prayer room

It wasn't until I sat down
On the prayer rug that I remembered
I was in Istanbul
The Idhan, call to prayer
Was being called from the masjid
I could see the lights of the minarets on
The hills in the distance

I close my eyes
Spiritual satisfaction
Overwhelmed me
Water filled my eyes

"Come to prayer, come to success"
Rang out from the voice of a Muslim brother
High up in the sky

We begin to make salat
My husband recited, "Al-Falaq"
The Daybreak, a Surah in the Quran
So fitting this morning
As the rain lightly fell outside
I could hear it in the background
A reminder of Allah

As-Salammu alaikum warahmatuallah
We turned to the right
As-salammu alaikum warahmatuallah
We turned to the left

I sat there for a spell
Asked for forgiveness
For patience with my children
And of course for a successful day of fasting

There is no easy way to
Explain the emotion
I feel like shouting
AllahuAkbar
G-d is the Greatest!
The feeling is breathtaking
And beyond any treasures of this life
A feeling beyond this world

Ramadan Karim
From Istanbul, TURKEY

Fajr Idhan

How can you sleep?
When I wake you by
Calling your soul back to me

G-d is the greatest, G-d is the greatest

It is not a dream
The beautiful sound ringing
In your ears

There is no G-d but me

Don't drift back to slumber
You are one that I have numbered
Open your eyes so you may see

Muhammad is my messenger

The light is just breaking
Across the sky
Wake up and be alive
It's time to profess your love for me

Come to Prayer

Can you hear me calling the achievers?

Come to Success

Be amongst the chosen true believers

Make haste to Prayer
G-d is the greatest; G-d is the greatest
There is no G-d but me

This morning Allah was my alarm clock
There is no feeling to explain,
Feeling that close to Allah (swt)
Last night my mind was very uneasy
And after I prayed Isha, the thoughts and voices left
I fell to sleep thinking of childhood memories
I called on him by his names
Ninety-nine names
And brought peace to my soul

Birlik Sokak, Levent, IST

I'm driving down Istanbul streets
Watching peddlers pedal
For their children to eat
While wrinkled rich ladies budge ahead in
Front of me and the children at the cinema line
Don't let this scarf and shade of my skin
Fool you for a second
I whisper within,
You don't know where I been!

I'm rolling down the streets of Istanbul
While young boys sell tissue
For pennies in the rain
Wheel chair rolls by, old
Man twisted up so, in pain
While his daughter recites Quran
Searching for charity through the bazaar's busy crowd
But none see them or hears her beautiful song
Through their
Gucci shades blinded by, Channel's double Cs

I'm riding down the streets of Istanbul
While bombs blast two minutes
From where they shampoo my hair
The walls shake as the bomb breaks
And divides the air
Children beg for thousands
While Bush visits Blair
Glass shatters everywhere

My baby girl unaware of death in the air

Next door my photos wait as
Cement walls fall
A day when the angels came to call and the
Trumpets made their sound
Twenty seven dead, four hundred injured
Riding through this town

I'm mobile on Istanbul streets
Watching minarets light up the sky in every direction
Every corner you turn calls a soul to prayer
Looking at boats sail
Across the sea, seven mountains watching
In the distance with me
Taxis swerve by buses packed
With a hard days worked smell
Cats running, poking noses
Into garbage bins, men
Singing the sale song of
Fruits and bakery while
Mister bucket man tries to hustle
Me for sixty million

When it rains, it pours
And the water runs down the seven hills
Sticky sweetwater cornbread
Which no one seems to be able to put down
Games won, candies gone
We ride, ride ride, Riding through this town

Last Page

Looking Back

Maybe one day
You will pack your bags
And find a space
Where no one will hurt you
Or let you down
Or lie, cheat, or steal
Take away everything you once
Thought to be true
Until then
Just read back through these pages
And see where you been
And ask yourself
If that's where you want to go

Biography

Jessica was born to a single mom in Minneapolis, Minnesota, attended a Black Panthers pre-school in Oakland, California, and returned at the age of five to the North side neighborhood of Minneapolis. She never met her biological father. Her mother's courage and her birth-father's Mississippi Delta genes all gave her a spunky determination that has brought her this far along her amazing journey. Poetry has been the way that Jessica has explored and sought to make sense of all the craziness that life brings with it. As she was first learning to read and write, her new adoptive father wrote poetry to reach out to her.

After overcoming the challenge of being expelled three months prior to graduation from De La Salle High School, Jessica still received her diploma and continued on to attend Hampton University in Virginia, founded in 1868 to educate former slaves. Now, raising five children she continues to pursue her education at Augsburg College. A senior majoring in Elementary Education with a math focus, she plans to eventually teach math in the inner city.

Married at the age of 19, a strong family and a sense of independence were two things that she dreamed about as a child. Woven through the threads of basketball and family has been her search for the meaning behind all the wins and losses, perfect shots and injuries. As a professional basketball player's wife, Jessica experienced both the realities of living the hoop dream, as well as the difficulties that come with being an athlete's wife. Learning to live with a husband on the road and trying to raise their growing family singly proved challenging.

Searching for truth and discipline, Jessica converted to Islam in 1996. Accepting the peace of Islam, in the community of Masjid An-Nur in North Minneapolis. Jessica has had the opportunity to see the world and loves to travel. Visiting places like Guatemala, India, and the Bahamas, and living in countries such as France, the Ukraine, and now Ankara, Turkey.

Like many other women, Jessica has been through many highs and lows of life and she has always been able to learn and grow and make each situation . . . well prosperous. As she recounts her experiences in love and life, she shares with us feelings and thoughts that I am sure every woman can relate to on some level. Through poetry, Jessica has found a way to tell her own stories. This first collection is painfully raw, often exposing her street smarts, idealism and sometimes naiveté'. It's a soul bearing glimpse into the unusual woman who is finding her own.